C🐾t Lovers Handbook

A storyteller book by
Nellie Edwards

To order additional copies of this book, contact:
Xlibris
844-714-8691
www.Xlibris.com
Orders@Xlibris.com

ISBN: Softcover   978-1-6698-5538-5
        Hardcover   978-1-6698-5539-2
        EBook   978-1-6698-5537-8

Library of Congress Control Number: 2022916773

Print information available on the last page

Rev. date: 11/17/2022

Cat Lovers Handbook

"If a baby won't come to you, look into your heart.
If a cat won't come to you, look into your soul."

Contents

Sheba

Sheba was a six-week old kitten that my daughter Leslie got from a rescue center, near her home in Gulfport, Florida. The people at the center gave her a container of Kitty Milk, a product designed for kittens that are too young for solid food and also told her the name of a pet shop where she could buy it. The next day, Leslie went to the shop where she purchased a supply of the pet milk. The woman in the store showed her a tiny bottle and nipple to use for the Kitty Milk. Leslie was very careful to feed the baby right on time and took Sheba to work with her, so the kitten soon got used to being around people. Sheba lived with Leslie for 20 years.

Leslie and her husband have another house in the country. Every few weeks, they would go to that house and Sheba went along. Sheba was an indoor cat and rarely went outside. One day, she decided to go out for a little sunshine. Leslie opened the door and out the cat went. She was sleeping quietly, curled up on the grass, when two big dogs from next door saw her. They came charging over to where she was, but then kept running. This was a strategy they had to make smaller animals, like cats, run, to then chase them down and kill them. Sheba was not about to run. Instead, she sat up, lifted her paw, stretched out her claws and hissed at them.

Inside the house, Leslie happened to be looking out the window and saw what was going on. She dashed out the door, scooped up the cat and ran back inside. She put her down and Sheba went calmly to get a drink of water, then got into her bed and went to sleep, undisturbed by the day's events.

Bless you, Sheba.

Snake Cat

One spring, a cat showed up right outside the kitchen screen door, at the house where I grew up. Because he was looking in the door, my mother assumed he was hungry, so she fed him. For the next couple of days, he ate twice a day outside that screen door. My mother thought he would go back where he came from, but my father said that a cat that had found food was not going to leave. By evening, the cat was gone. But not forever.

Before too long, around ten one morning, the cat showed up again, only this time, he was not alone. In his mouth, he had a snake. My mother was horrified. The snake was alive, but the cat had broken its back and it couldn't crawl away. The snake had become a toy. Later that day, the cat killed the snake, and ate it. This was a way of life for the cat, and this habit of his continued the rest of the spring.

Our way of life was to leave home every summer and go to the beach, to stay in a family cottage located on Anna Maria Island. Since the cat could feed himself catching snakes, we left him behind. Sure enough, when we returned at the end of summer, the cat was still there.

The cat lived with us for a number of years, but finally, the last year, when we came back from the beach, he was nowhere to be found. We imagined that he had been bitten by a rattlesnake, since he had once brought one of these home. We could never expect to have such a unique cat again.

By the way, this cat never came when he was called, but among ourselves, we called him Blue.

Sunshine

It was a beautiful day. Albert and I were ready to leave Florida on a trip out West. We hadn't made plans to stop overnight, thinking we would just stop wherever we were, whenever we felt like it. Later that afternoon, we spotted a chain motel and pulled in. I went in to see if they had space and how much it would cost. The rate was right and they had only one room left. We decided to stay. The café had good food; we ate and went to bed. We had a parking space right out the room's front door, so we parked the truck there. They even had a night watchman.

The next morning, we got up at nine and went down to eat breakfast. Once we were finished, I packed the bags. Albert was shaving, so I told him I'd go down and check us out, which I did. I went out to the truck with a bag when I saw a woman and a little boy, about four year's old, standing by our truck. As I approached them, the little boy asked, "Is this your truck." To which I answered yes. His mother said, "There's a kitten in there," pointing up under the bed of the truck. Sure enough, crouched under the truck was a small yellow kitten.

I set down the bag I was carrying and said, "Someone has thrown this kitty out. I'll have to catch it." I walked up to the side of the truck and called the kitty. She looked at me, and moved farther back under the truck. I walked away, and the kitty came out. This was repeated three times before I said, "I've got do something different here."

I said to the little boy, "Will you watch the kitty to see where it goes," and then to the mother, "Don't let him try to catch it, it may bite."

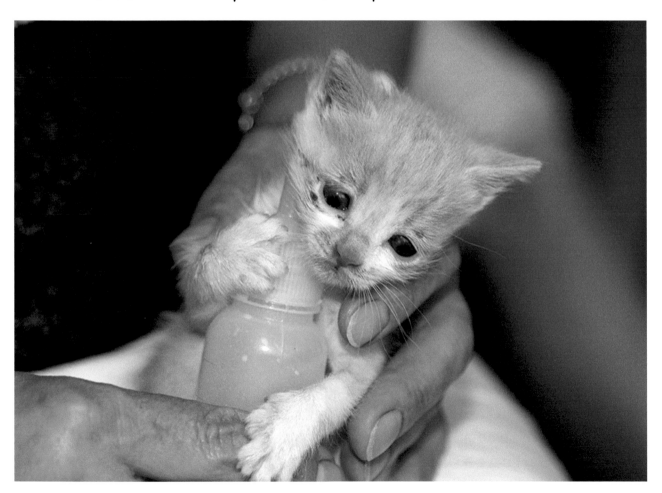

Next, I went to the office and after telling the man at the counter about the problem, I told him I needed a cardboard box big enough for the kitten, with an old towel to put in the bottom, plus a paper bowl and two small cartons of milk. He called the kitchen and asked them to bring him these items.

The yard man came in with the box asking what it was for. The woman from the kitchen arrived with the milk. They were both curious about what was going on, so we told them. The woman said, "You don't have to worry about a home for the kitten, my husband and I have a small farm where we live. I'm seeing mice and I need a cat." I said that would be fine, but with one promise: "Name the cat Sunshine."

This town only keeps abandoned pets for two weeks and we didn't want the kitty to die. Sunshine would become a farm cat.

I went back out to the truck with the items they had given me, opened the milk, poured it into the paper bowl and, with my right hand, placed it on the girder under the truck, but kept hold of it. I placed my other hand just to the left of the kitten and wouldn't move it again until I caught her. With my right hand, I moved the bowl a bit closer to the kitty and called her. I could see her sniffing the air. It was the milk. She came a little closer and I moved the bowl closer to her. She could resist no more and crept over to the bowl to lap up the milk. That was when I swiftly moved my left hand to the back of her neck and grabbed her.

Goodbye, Sunshine. Enjoy the farm life!

Cat Trucker

Albert and I were traveling out West on a major highway in a double line of traffic which was moving slowly forward. As I looked to the left, in the other lane, I saw the driver of a semi-truck with a cat draped around his neck. I said to Albert, "Look!" and pointed toward the trucker. The man driving the truck noticed Albert looking at him. He smiled and moved on ahead. A couple of miles down the road, we saw his blinker turn on. Albert said, "The truck's getting off. We need to eat and get gas." So, we turned off the highway.

When we got out, the trucker was standing on a small patch of grass to our right, watching the cat do her business. Albert walked over and said to him, "Your cat's a real friend. How did this start?" The man responded, "Just like today, I stopped to get gas and saw a small kitten by the door to the dining room, very frightened. I thought she was hungry, so I picked her up, took her in with me to eat. I ordered my food, and I told the server I also needed a paper bowl and a child- sized carton of milk. When she brought my order, I placed the bowl on the floor, poured some of the milk into it and sat the kitty down by the bowl.

The kitten smelled the milk and immediately began to lap it up. I finished eating and we left. As we started down the road in the truck, she tried to get in my lap. I picked her up and put her on my shoulder. She snuggled down, very much at home, and we went on to deliver our load.

When I go home and take time off, she's happy to be there. She loves my wife and family, but when I start getting ready to leave, she understands what I'm doing and won't let me out of her sight. She's ready to hit the road again. I used to get lonely, but not anymore. She's been riding with me for eight years now.

A Cat's Favorite Food

Cats love fish. It can be canned or fresh and they will catch their own, if they have a chance. What they will do first is find a good spot, a pond or stream where there is shallow water with small fish. They wait and watch, until one appears, then scoop it up with a paw, sending the fish to the ground, swipe it again, knocking it farther from the water, to then settle down to eat their catch. This is repeated three or four times, but the last fish will be taken home. There may be a mate and kittens there, or the fish may be eaten the next day for breakfast.

You can see this ability in action if you have a goldfish bowl or an aquarium.

Mystery Cat

This story took place where I live, in Cassadaga, Florida, which has become known as a cat refuge, so we have lots of cats in the neighborhood. There was an elderly couple living down the street from Albert and I. Both were cat lovers. Sadly, the wife was bedridden, but the man took wonderful care of her, bathing and cooking for her.

One day, she asked him to get her a new cat. Hers had passed away. He went to the local cat shelter and brought home a beautiful white kitten. His wife was delighted. After her lunch, she would take a nap and the husband would take the kitten with him out onto the porch to sit in his lap, in the sun. A couple hours later, his wife would wake up and he would take the cat back in to be with her. This was a regular pattern.

Unexpectedly, the man died. I knew, when this happened, that the wife would not live long and she didn't. Now the cat had no one, so our neighbor Richard across the street took him in, even installing a cat door for his new furry friend.

A month or so later, Albert was out in front of our house. The white cat ran up to him and began rubbing his leg. Albert glanced over at me and said, "Look at this." The cat followed him to our front door and watched him go into the house.

The next day, we were bringing in some groceries and left the door open. We got back into the kitchen and here comes the cat. He runs around, goes back into the reading room, out into the living room, past the fireplace and up the stairs. I went to get him just in time to see the cat go into the front bedroom, circle around, come out and go into the back bedroom, look into the TV room, then down the stairs again and out the front door. He ran over to the curb, looked both ways, zipped across the street and went straight through the cat door. Now I have seen dogs look for traffic this way, but never before a cat.

Now every chance he gets, the white cat comes over for his tour of our house. We love him.

Postscript

Here's a picture of me in Utah with Flagerman, the best dog ever and a cat lover, too.

Printed in the United States
by Baker & Taylor Publisher Services